AMERICAN GRAVITY
By
SHEILA M. ALEXANDER

AMERICAN GRAVITY
Copyright © 2018 Sheila M. Alexander
Lady Word Publishing
ISBN-13: 978-0-692-04551-0

No part of this book may be used or reproduced in any manner whatsoever without the written consent of Sheila M. Alexander. For information address ladyworddesign@outlook.com
Printed in the United States of America

Table of Contents

HOLD AMERICA	1
LIGHT TO A DARK CULTURE	2
WARS AND RUMORS	3
SCRAMBLED	4
FREEDOM'S EXPRESSION	6
FREEDOM	7
AMERICA THE BEAUTIFUL	8
THE POLITICAL HUSTLE	10
THE RALLY	11
FREEDOM WITHIN THE WALLS	12
CANDIDATE'S NOTION	13
WHAT FOR	14
STOP THE SILENCE - ANTI-BULLY	15
THE MONSTER IN THE CLOSET	16
RAPE	17
HATE	18
DOUBLE STANDARD	19
WONDER BLUES	20
THE WAY IT IS	21
BULLIED	22
LOST IN TIME	23
THE SEARCH	24
CULPRIT EXTINCTION	25
AN ENEMY	26
IDENTITY	27
WHAT WAY	28
AMERICA'S PRIDE	29
FALLING NATION	30
LIBERTY	31

FADING	32
WAR OF THE WORDS	33
ELEPHANTS AND ASSES	34
FEMINISM	35
INFORM AND POLLUTE	36
DEVICES	37
FOOLISH VOTES	38
INSIDE OUT OPINION	39
EDUCATIONAL DEBATE	40
CAMPAIGNING	41
IMMIGRATION	42
IMPLOSION	43
PO-LIGHT	44
BAD BLUE POINT OF VIEW	46
OPEN FORUM	47
TROUBLED WATER	48
FOUNDING	49
BLACK POWERLESS	50
"O" REALLY	51
TROLLS	52
GOLDEN SNUBS	53
SAME FACE DEMONS	54
VIOLENT VICTORY	55
BE STRONG	56
BANNERS	57
SOLUTIONS	58
GUNS	59
EMERGENCY	60
HELP MY SHAME	61
REFLECTIONS ON THE GROUND	62
OUTLINES IN THE ROAD	64
QUESTION OF FATE	65
NOT FORGOTTEN	66

THE PEOPLE'S GOVERNMENT Part 1	68
THE PEOPLE'S GOVERNMENT Part 2	69
TRAPPED	70
THE BLACKNESS	72
FRIENEMY	73
SLAVERY	74
WHITE REFLECTION	76
EXCLUSION	78
MURDEROUS DEVOTION	80
SHADOW MEN	81
BEYOND THE WALLS	82
REASONABLE ANGER	83
LOVE DIVIDE	86
POLITICAL IMPOTENCE	87
BLOODY DIRECTION	88
NO CHARGE	90
LIKE NO OTHER	92
IN CONTRAST	94
A GREAT NATION	95
BEGIN AGAIN	96
NATIVE DESTINY	97
KEEP HOPE	98
LOST AT HOME	99
BEHIND THE LINES	100
LOST	101
AWAY DEMOCRACY	102
BEAR BEWARES	103
CHOICES	104
A PRESENT PAST	105
HOPELESS TIME	106
STROKES OF PAIN	107
SCRAMBLED LINES	108
PRECIOUS FOOL	109

ALLEGIANCE	110
CONFLICTS	111
GAS BY TRAGEDY	112
RAGING STORMS	114
THE MADNESS	116
REIGNING DARK DAYS	117
BUCKETS AND BOATS	118
INDECENT BEHAVIORS	119
SILENCE OF THE MAN	120
SEXUAL ENTITLEMENT	121
THE NEVER ENDING STORY	122
ADDICTED	123
GOVERNMENT'S DEPENDENCY	124
ABORTION	125
LEFT BEHIND	126
FAITH AND PATRIOTISM	127
LOVE SURVIVES	128

HOLD AMERICA
Yearnings for America strong
Rebuild the pride for us to stand
The vision strong but hope deferred
Division spread across the land

LIGHT TO A DARK CULTURE

A cultural darkness foundation laid
Silence the value of money paid
Quiet emotions and actions undone
Truth in the closet the payment has shunned

Light had to shadow the cultural norms
Under concealment perpetual storms
Preying on chances to stroke a vile pride
Power the husband influence the bride

Claims were offensive no one would believe
Dance in the sun was the way to deceive
Feeding a monster with silence and smiles
Increased its hunger and made it worthwhile

But bursting abundance has shattered the days
Pull back the covers the hunter's betrayed
Lifting the windows and opening doors
Showing the secrets the victims have stored

Actions appalling to what was perceived
Family and colleagues are left to bereave
Pain was the vessel that harvested light
Reaping a voice say goodbye to the night

WARS AND RUMORS

Monsters that once crept in the dark
Are now dancing in the light
Quiet was the war within
But now it takes a stand to fight

Shooting stars that burst demise
Tease the watchers braced to stare
Gripping throats with threats of strength
Friends bewildered how to care

Flexing muscles to be first
Lips too loose to firm the fight
Hate is rendered with precision
Light has captured fear of night

Power is the tug of war
Death the finish of the game
Straddled fences some embrace
Pride and glory brought to shame

SCRAMBLED
Loss of vision
Glass in the eyes
Path is darkened
River is dried
Stuck in the mud
Feet tightly bound
Falling in darkness
A whole in the ground

Passionate screams
Voices are loud
Chanting and ranting
A vigorous crowd
Emotional highs
Morale sinking low
Executives scribing
A heart wrenching blow

Chaos uniting
Drawing the lines
Sessions of hatred
Recalling the time
Peace is a myth
War is the way
Love under pressure
To hurt and to stray

People forgotten
Cities are lost
Survival the fittest
And life is the cost
Solutions are twisted
Government fails
The people's republic
On course won't prevail

FREEDOM'S EXPRESSION
Pride dancing in the streets
Fists pounding in the air
Flags waving glories past
Hatred spilling everywhere

Suffered passions tears do flow
Voices clashing cross the lines
Aggravated hopes don't know
Burning stripes and picket signs

Truth is fatal lies survive
Faith is broken in the pain
Answers waning in the present
Future questions what's to gain

<u>FREEDOM</u>
Fighting For
Redemption's Reign
Enduring Effort's
Everlasting Effect
Democratic Dominance
Opening Opportunities
Made Manifest

AMERICA THE BEAUTIFUL
They're all created equal
Happiness liberty justice for all
But they're lustful eye and pride of life
Contribute to her fall

Her shores that beckoned hope
Now drenched with fear and hate
Security challenges freedom
Her government plays with fate

Her people create divides
All in the name of rights
Love religion and race
The core reasons that they fight

Prosperity favors a few
And poverty seems to flourish
The rules and regulations
Those with money they seem to nourish

Peace a rare condition
Violence having its way
Anger in gun debates
To keep or take away

Disrespect is scoring high
Accountability is low
Rapist running rampant
Moral values they don't show

Murder and bigotry
Seem to dominate her days
Deceit and degradation
Are the characters that they play

America they love
In her name they take a stand
Their proclamation strong
But their ways defame her brand

Resting in her arms
Are promises of old
Crying out for justice
But her honor they have sold

America the beautiful
Her people have forgotten
They're bringing her to shame
A dimming light her words downtrodden

THE POLITICAL HUSTLE
Fatten desire with sugary lies
Blind and lead them all astray
Feed their will with false hope
Dependency will surely stay

Excite emotions drowning fear
Whip them with a hurtful past
Appeasing with indulging will
Take their wants for needs to last

Paint the road with fool's gold
Give direction twisted trails
In a circle minds will mold
Cultivated votes won't fail

THE RALLY

Victims chanting a crazed praise
Predatory drives peak to advance
Spells are cast with promising terms
Mouths devouring innocent souls

Eyes deceitfully smiling truth
Egos soar at bowing minds
Agendas swell at passing hands
Worlds of pain awaits beyond

FREEDOM WITHIN THE WALLS
The liability
Is that humans cannot be trusted
Freedom will be used
To hurt and abuse
And then we'll lose
What's been bled for
Consequences for man's actions
Are mere distractions
'Cause responsibility is a low commodity
Freedom has no reigns in man's mind
To be hateful or kind
His decision without a care
No matter when no matter where
No matter how much it costs
Freedom will be a downfall
For all that know not what it means
That care less for its value and its claim
To be free and not understand the name
Under which we all stand
We'll be like sheep taking a brand
Free to roam in our pen
Blinded by the wall
Though there's more than what's within

CANDIDATE'S NOTION

Voters are addicted to hope
Because truth lives only in words
Fulfilled by thoughts and dreams never seen
Intoxicating wishful thinking the truth becomes blurred

Rejection of the truth without thought
For hope is fulfilling on emotional planes
Truth near extinction and harder to swallow
Because with it may come sorrow or pain

And to the voters notion
Hope is all that is needed for survival of mankind
By the masses they gather for another dose
Lying lips serve the potion injected by crafty minds

WHAT FOR

Retaliation to the uniform
This is the time for unity
But there's an immunity
To love
Hate is blind in front view
It only sees black or blue
And so they attack
Gunning each other down
With ill purpose no slack
Create a media circus
Antagonizing hurt
Jumping both sides of the fence
Wishing the grass was greener
Under a bridge never crossed
And lives continue to be lost
Waiting for workable solutions
But revolutions
Are the crop in the garden
Reaping a harvest full of blood
And a great divide
Tears flowing on either side
When will it come to an end
And the lives of all be easy to defend
We're creating insanity
And in the midst of all
We are losing our humanity

STOP THE SILENCE - ANTI-BULLY

Stop the madness the pressure the pain
Be a voice in the midst of disdain
Walking by disregarding what's real
Hiding eyes so you don't have to feel

Suffering in the view of behind
Silence says you are some-what aligned
Bullying is the stance that one takes
Suffering is the bed that one makes

For another it's grief and despair
Searching eyes wishing someone was there
To lend a voice and a hand in accord
Making known that these deeds are abhorred

Stop the silence the violence is real
Take a stand with courageous appeal
Make it known bullying has to cease
Tear it down let the pressure release

Silence kills there is no other choice
Change can come with a positive voice
Loud and clear band together unite
Using words as a positive light

Understand that it can't be ignored
'Cause suicide is its painful reward
Break the silence and make all aware
Life is dependent there's no time to spare

THE MONSTER IN THE CLOSET

There's a monster in the closet
Heed the warning stay away
His agenda is perversion
And he craves invasive play

Hands reach out to grab you
Or to swipe you from behind
Touching all the secrets
He was never meant to find

Lips that press for pleasure
Whisper lies and vulgar tales
Wet with eager passion
And with kisses that assail

Tongue with filthy talent
Seeking hope to forge ahead
Satisfy the hunger
Lusting for forbidden bread

Mastermind the pendulum
That sits between his thighs
Feed his bloated ego
As he takes what's been denied

His culture is a brotherhood
That's silently indorsed
His pedestals are women
Funded silence fear enforced

Broken
Frightened
Lost
Ashamed

Guilty
Alone
Invisible
Defamed

Powerless
Dirty
Confused
Dazed

Abandoned
Hurt
Ugly
Crazed

Depressed
Trapped
Helpless
Abused

Sickened
Lifeless
Disgraced
Used

RAPE

HATE

The darkness within permeates surrounding life
Harvesting vessels and victims with blood
Overwhelming hearts with its vile infection
As vulgar voices declare its creed

Victims moan at the sight left behind
Innocence trembles in the waves of its steps
The Faith-full fall from the weight of its hand
And hope is lost for the targeted souls

DOUBLE STANDARD

The hatred no one will pursue
Blacks are prejudice too
In fact they're worse
We live under their curse
Affirmative action
A major infraction
To deny us
For the color of their skin
Slavery a constant weapon
To whip the present
Having to bow for the sake of their shame
Incapable of honoring their ancestor's name
Instead they complain
And we continue to open doors
In which they refuse to walk
Because they're blinded by their own hate
Sealing their fate
With a pitiful pride
They fail themselves
And dish us the blame

WONDER BLUES
Blue tears kiss the cheeks of sorrow
Blue cries pierce the open air
Blue hearts ache and long for solace
Blue hands grasp a friend in despair
Blue arms open to hold the broken
Blue words lift a time once known
Blue love soothes the hardship taken
Blue lives ransom by giving their own

THE WAY IT IS

A legal extermination in our nation
Justification inscribed on the uniform
White faces and black bodies a horrendous mix
Authorities wink an eye at the perpetual storm

Confidence in laws that are flawed
Applied by one sided minds and crooked hearts
No intentions for justice only satisfaction
When a black man falls and death parades start

White and blue a combination that is deadly and true
The appraisal of black skin declared worthless to a dime
Indignation and grief couples lies and twisted words
Assumed legislation is that black males are the crime

BULLIED

Every morning filled with dread and anxiety
To wake and rise a misery and shame
Fear overtakes the familiar unknown
Being who I am the only reason to blame

Battered by words and plagued by memories
Cut by stares of the passers-by
Teasing an art they have mastered so well
The use of words I have grown to despise

Standing alone and sitting in agony
Nobody dares to take up my cross
Swallowing pain is my only dignity
Resistance declares my certain loss

LOST IN TIME

Detrimental moments
Quakes from the grave
Cries from old blood
Tears from bruised feet

Lost in changing sounds
Vision deprived of victory
Democratic collision
Walls crumble in submission

Liberty stoops low
Security plaguing peace
Justice immorally weighed
Pride fed by greed

THE SEARCH
A fearless pursuit to make America great again
Faithful hearts grasping for the beat of hope again
Discerning eyes looking for the vision of pride again
Daring spirits rising to the call to fight again

CULPRIT EXTINCTION
Black on black crime
LGBT bashing
Vindicated rapist
Races clashing

Pulpit molesters
Cyber hackers
Social media trolls
Terrorist attackers

Governmental greed
Deficient education
Welfare minds
Excessive legislation

Religious wars
National debt
Polluted shores
Mistreated vets

The healthcare system
Prejudice police
Cultural denial
Tax increase

Refusing to vote
Media fabrications
Forgotten pasts
The nation's segregation

AN ENEMY
Standing on the foot of a wealthy nation
Is one that is angry troubled and confused
The weight of their view
Torments the souls of peace
And disrupts the harmony of truth and justice

There foot is stayed
Determined to strip away strength
Using time to wear down patience and pride
With threats and violence
They crack firm foundations
Plaguing the weak with false ideals and philosophies

IDENTITY
I can change my gender
But not my race
Between my legs voice chest and face
I have free reign

WHAT WAY

Some disagree at the possibility
That born is not the reality
But birth declares what's beneath the skin

LGBT is not about sexuality
But soul identity
Who one is—is called from within

AMERICA'S PRIDE

Waving in a silent breeze
Ripples dance in freedom's arms
Bold in color standing tall
Saluting victories from all harm

Wave your flag oh country strong
Let its strength breathe life anew
Wave your flag the whole day long
Wave it proud the tried and true

Gracing walls where scholars learn
Gracing final resting grounds
Gracing souls that on it yearn
Gracing halls our fathers found

Wave your flag oh country strong
Let its strength breathe life anew
Wave your flag the whole day long
Wave it proud the tried and true

The price was blood that made it so
Divided hearts that toiled and fought
But once revealed from skies a glow
United as the hope was sought

Wave your flag oh country strong
Let its strength breathe life anew
Wave your flag the whole day long
Wave it proud the tried and true

FALLING NATION

Losing feathers during flight
Trapped inside a raging wind
To find the sun nowhere in sight
Struggling sorely to ascend

The wings of justice quickly fail
Shrieking for salvations hand
With hope a friendship would prevail
And feet on peace to safely stand

The heart of pride is beating fast
And quickly dwindles faith and trust
Flashes from a hopeful past
Reject assurance strength and thrust

Land appears and fear takes hold
Inside the fight is sure and brutal
Falling shows a fate so cold
The life that was now seems so futile

LIBERTY

Liberty's stipulation is that you follow the rules
Freedom isn't free unless you pay the penalty
Of staying within its borders
Boundaries etched in the word unseen
But without them freedom is flawed
Standing straight and tall
Marked within the walls
Of justice
Freedom demands that we follow the law
Subjection to the law frees one
From it all

FADING

Impotent efforts failing generations before
Time's resolutions fade perseverance
Discipline a rarity weakening the cause
What cries are heard in the distant past

Blood shed diluted forgotten in vanity
Selfish pride has distorted the view
The future bargained for material gain
Shadows uncertain today's action cost

WAR OF THE WORDS

Incredible passion displayed on the stage
As viable contenders with words they do wage
Conviction and confidence laced with pride
With money and slander their purpose does ride

Supporters are raging and eating the vibe
Fulfilling a destiny fools would prescribe
A violent respect is the tribute that's handed
Political right is the tool that is branded

Opponents strike hard with past acts fore fronted
Combatting their wounds with scandals they've hunted
And citizens wait in the wings of contention
Debating the issues contenders won't mention

The answers unknown to the critical matters
Core values degraded foundation is shattered
The carnage outstanding vile words with finesse
With smiles to the office the hopefuls do press

ELEPHANTS AND ASSES

Progression stunted and pride is lost
Elephants and Asses bumbling about
Dependently trampling over great beyond
Writing the future an endless doubt

Elephants stampede at the thought of change
Their only remembrance is what once was
Asses relentless to make a new face
Evolving with passion a thunderous cause

Pissing and bucking on each other's turf
Leaving bewildered a hopeless folk
Civil concessions unheard and refused
Binding the peoples with pen-less strokes

Treading destruction and butting heads
Forgetting the vows and oaths once sworn
Stubbornly standing on broken grounds
Representing beliefs self-shattered and torn

FEMINISM

She can do it too
Absolutely even better
The world - a piece of cake
If only men would stop and let her

Issues sure resolved
And all who breathe would finally see
A woman is the answer
Unapologetically

INFORM AND POLLUTE

Media manipulates and masters
The twisting of lies with facts
Reporting such a program that's partisan
The right to know a tool to distract

The beguiling and defrauding of the people
To prey on simple proud and weak
Perpetuating cycles of emotions
Inciting rage with faulty words they speak

The spectrum of their reach is broad
Filling ears seizing unsettled minds
Creating atmospheres contentious and vile
Riling the public its intentional design

There's no truth to lights camera action
The people deserve to be informed
Agendas money and political ploys
That's what is spewed and proudly performed

DEVICES
Pulling down the stronghold of America
Create diversions that will force divides
Strip away the vital founding portion
Leave her in the ash of greed and pride

FOOLISH VOTES

The American voter
Blind ignorance to truth
Eyes wide shut
Closed to the reality
Or maybe denial
That controls the hand
And dilutes the mind
Or could it be worse
The wanted truth of
Confusion and destruction
A new America
Built on the backs of the impotent
Designed by evil fools

INSIDE OUT OPINION

The American people
Driven by greed and violence
Trampling the tombs of forefathers
Ignoring the whispers in the silence

The American people
Thinking they are wise but fools
Divided yet claiming their strength
Using decaying wealth as a tool

The American people
Killing their own without war
Freedom is traded for egos glory
Constitutional founding gutted to the core

The American people
Preach the world philosophy vein
Dying from the inside out
Stripes are shredded and stars do wane

EDUCATIONAL DEBATE

We debate education
Raise tuition or make it free
Student loans an educational groan
Degrees and debt together entwined

We debate education
As teachers strike for higher pay
Class rooms fold to mice and mold
So to the streets the scholar's assigned

We debate education
While our children's thoughts roam
Taking tests and finding they're less
Than the world's brilliant minds

We debate education
With books antique and worn
And the cost - our students are lost
In the agenda of political grind

CAMPAIGNING

All the people sway
To the twisting of minds with cunning vows
Treacherous hearts pasty smiles
As their pockets they endow

Shaking hands with their victims
Tainted fingers fill the grasp
Egos flaring deceitful eyes
Lips lashing lying tongues as voter's hopes they clasp

IMMIGRATION
Immigration legislation
Who comes who goes who stays
The solution can be found in the Constitution
But interpreters lack knowledge
No understanding
No wisdom for a resolution

IMPLOSION

Sinking fast in its blood soaked sands
Starved bodies and poverty survives
Murderous voices chant the nations call
A melting pot of bitter souls connive

Selfish greed feeding double faces
Time is spilled on dead hopes and dreams
Reckless lives celebrating priceless freedom
Divided falls praising united schemes

PO-LIGHT
Faithful protector
Neighborhood friend
Serving the people
Their safety defend

Community icon
With honor they fight
Patrolling the days
And guarding the nights

Dangerous places
The call sometimes leads
To violent people
They have to proceed

Their lives although precious
They must not draw back
They'll face much resistance
And vicious attacks

Some days will bring joy
Their hand they will give
To help one in need
Or push one to live

Their labor is endless
Their duty for peace
Committed to justice
Their drive does not cease

The oath they uphold
Integrity too
Is bound in their blood
That humbly flows blue

BAD BLUE POINT OF VIEW
Black faces perfect bullseye
Bullets pierce bodies convulse
Shadows of hatred played in the light
Fear of the flashes a racing pulse

Magnum revolver crowned prince
Extinguish the vile existence at hand
Stomp out the breath of useless creatures
Death is the hope and hate is the brand

OPEN FORUM
Voters protest
Fists and elbows
Fighting opposers
Prejudice blows
Anger and hatred
Driving the mass
Political venues
Holding the class
Shouting and blaming
Societies crash
Cities and towns
Behold the backlash
Uniting the public
A vicious divide
The office beheld
As the people collide

TROUBLED WATER
The city's water
Poisons sons and daughters
And victims foot the bill
For what taints and makes them ill

Lifelong problematic
Careless deeds or systematic
Trapped inside aquatic hell
Drowning dreams at every cell

Plastic bottles regrets and speeches
Won't erase the permanent reaches
Innocent cries the fear for future
Shots and serums cannot suture

Clean the waters closed eyes converse
Won't reverse the drinkable curse
What a quandary a life changing case
The pitiful city on its citizens did place

FOUNDING

The Christian portrayal of what should be
Values and morals and equality
Loving thy brother forgiving the wrong
Makes a great country and its people strong

Faith is the founder of principles great
Fore fathers and brothers our country create
To stand under wings of ideals that last
Engrained in the image of governments past

On stone and on paper across the land
Reminding the people of where to stand
To hold to the cause and vision defended
And praise to the justice and truth commended

BLACK POWERLESS

When blacks assume positions of authority
Everyone does an about face
Agendas plans budgets proposals
All seem to tumble at a quick pace

The care the attention the focus and hard work
Tip out the door with suspicious hands
The drive progression and vision for more
Take a bow and commence to disband

Is it the change the face or the unfamiliar
That corrupts the office when blacks lead
Or is it the act of others that plot their defeat
In hopes that they would quickly concede

"O" REALLY

Did he orchestrate the racial divide
Did he wave his hand and the people collide
Did he hate this country so
That he would start a war on the low

Was the fame of White House grand
Reason enough to take command
Did he let our enemies roam
In the place that we call home

Could one accomplish feats so bold
Expose the country to fail and fold
Did political power go to his head
Did he sabotage government and leave it for dead

Did he use a pen to destroy what was made
Are his roots the cause for how he is swayed
Did he do it all like so many accuse
Or was it all a political rouse

TROLLS

How opinionated you can be
When your face they cannot see
Verbal clashes racist rants
Hateful words and violent chants

On a keyboard you are strong
Face the screen the whole day long
But truth be told you're merely this
A waste of time in endless bliss

GOLDEN SNUBS

A system divided glistening gold
Rewarding the worthy arms do fold
With anticipation standing tall
A great nomination as he calls

With pride and acceptance waiting near
A glory and honor to hold him dear
Counted a member upon the greats
Academy tenders the winning fate

All of the faces filled with smiles
Waiting the moment to walk the aisle
Accepting the statue defining the craft
But under the glory beholds a down draft

Swept to the side of his great stance
A whole world of people forbidden the chance
With giftings and skill most second to none
Are people of color the system has shunned

They fill the arenas box office climbs high
They bring on the laughter they make us all cry
They act with compassion our hearts they do touch
Perfecting the art that we love so much

But blind to the minds of the powers that be
Refused and ignored intentionally
Though good for the money they harvest with talent
Denied recognition the system unbalanced

SAME FACE DEMONS
Murderous Muslims and belligerent blacks
Justify the hatred and vicious attacks
Detest and slander religious conviction
Trapped in a cycle of violent addictions

Killing each other and slaying the masses
All in the name of faith and past clashes
Blood is the solvent to rid what opposes
Cased in a cause that terror discloses

Walking the streets and shopping the malls
Innocent victims will answer the calls
Leaving despair as questions assemble
And demonize those whose look hate resembles

VIOLENT VICTORY
The bravery of blatant violence
Piercing terror in to the silence
Placing fear on every face
Dividing worlds by faith and race
Giving victory to hatred's fueled alliance

BE STRONG

The audacity of bloody victims
Searching out the violent calls
Looking for the twisted reasons
Hailing those that death befalls

How dare you challenge fear
Gaze your enemy in the eye
Create a stance of opposition
Refuse defeat refuse to die

Why do you keep resisting
Hate with vigor will succeed
For this cause requires life
And its mission you won't impede

But you keep pressing on
Fierce and stronger than before
Letting time and peace unfold
And hope and faith in time restore

BANNERS

Bloody banners high and free
Dancing in the breeze
With hope and value paint the skies
From power that was seized

Draping tombs in fields of plenty
Leaving tearful stains
Crumbled in the minds of those
Its colors have brought pain

Folded in an honored box
For those who gave their lives
Dressed upon the backs of those
Who use it to bring strife

Bloody banners trampled on
By those who've lost its trust
Stitched upon the arm of those
Whose loyalty's a must

Framed within the hearts of those
Whose freedom it did buy
Snuggled in the arms of those
Whose faith on it relies

SOLUTIONS

Are efforts for peace useless
Is the world doomed for worse
Will poverty cease to exist for all
Are we trapped in an Earthly curse

Will war always be the answer
Are governments destined to fail
Will races embrace segregation
Will hate and prejudice prevail

Will bellies now empty be filled
Will those who are trapped be free
Are cures for diseases kept secret
Will countries ever agree

Is money the source of true freedom
Does fame indicate you exist
Is value only measured by numbers
Will religious violence persist

Is murder the name for abortion
Are guns to blame for their use
Can gender be rightfully changed
Is spanking a form of abuse

Will answers be found in the wise
Will societies find their resolve
Does anyone care for solutions
Will issues forever evolve

GUNS

Lifeless Objects

People lack control

Causing death

Guns

EMERGENCY

Twisted metal burned by fuel of hate
Sounds of thunder bodies from windows escape
Frosted faces ashes of past existence
Corrupted planes weapons of hates persistence

Flashing lights rescuers racing fast
Screaming voices hunting salvation's path
Tumbling buildings darkening clouds avail
Growing silence from the noise prevails

Perfect strangers lending helping hands
Pleading hearts prayers across the land
Bonding peoples in resolve unite
Standing together against terror they fight

HELP MY SHAME

Self esteem void
Living in agony
Battered words
Losing my sanity

Questioning life
And what I'm supposed to be
Dreading the days
And begging for amnesty

Walking alone
My only security
Building a wall
Deflecting hostility

Crying in silence
For what has become of me
Looking for hope
And hidden immunity

Lost in a crowd
Invisible mockery
Eyes though they stare
Acknowledging shame of me

Shrink to the size
Of how I feel inwardly
Banish this life
And bury my misery

REFLECTIONS ON THE GROUND

Reflections on the ground
Spreading terror to the masses
Bloody puddles run
Through the streets like molasses
Sugar coating hate
And seducing thoughts of crime
Prepping for the next
Cause there isn't any time
For peace in the moment
Hope to settle what disturbs
Instead it rages on
Making war at every curb
Violence is the norm
Every mouth has an excuse
Blame it on the other
Cause destruction's running loose
Terrorizing mothers
Ripping neighborhoods apart
Dividing what was broken
Shedding light on hidden hearts
Revealing evil truths
That for some hard to believe

While others had the knowledge
And some practiced to deceive
A shadow ever present
Haunting everyone involved
A law could not erase
Nor could time and space dissolve
A horrid solid fact
That we've never been united
The writing in the books
And the words of man recited
Couldn't slay this truth
Hate has always had it's place
Destroying hopeful lands
For belief lifestyle and race
Fueled by pride and lies
Peace is driven to the grave
Buried in the dark
For destruction to enslave
Freedom rings aloud
But the ears that hear are bound
To the destiny of hate
More reflections on the ground

OUTLINES IN THE ROAD
Stroking chalk to the ground
A jagged frame of senseless death
Uniting outlined brothers

Tortured souls walk about
Suffering over the cold
Screams of torment weeping mothers

Anger grabs the moments
Bleeding streets bare witness
Society divides responsibility denied

Justice fiercely demanded
Analyzed through picketing signs
Accusations hurled to every side

Questions reversed confusion
Solutions lost in grappling hands
Comprehension fizzles in agony

Disagree and deviate
Subtly sway unsteady attention
Passing time quietly erases tragedy

Hands up quickly running
Gasping for every breath
To the ground bodies smother

Facing fear from end to end
Just by chance or ill intent
Another joins the outlined brothers

QUESTION OF FATE
A Beacon bright with hope
A fading star in night
A fire without heat and light

Infected from afar
Plagued by a friend
Conquered by the troubles within

America is great they claim
Some say it used to be
While others say it never was - undeniably

NOT FORGOTTEN

Bearing the sorrow
Embracing the cries
Duffle in hand
They said their good-byes

With courage and honor
They took on the plight
Relying on training
To give them insight

Dig to the ground
And take to the air
Flow through the waters
And make them aware

The warriors here
And they're full of pride
For flag and country
They brace them inside

Prepared for the battle
They pushed full force
While facing their rivals
They held to the course

The enemy tried
To break their resolve
But passion and will
They could not dissolve

Focused determined
To win for their land
Braving the strike
With weapon in hand

Pleading the cause
With each move they made
Fierce and forceful
They would not be swayed

Giving their all
Beginning to end
Victory's won
For all they defend

Blood on the shores
And dirt soaked within
Leaving the proof of
Where bravery has been

The warrior's cry
Let not it be lost
The people protected
With their life it cost

THE PEOPLE'S GOVERNMENT Part 1

Democracy shredded by well-oiled machines
Sweet liberty barren from her breast they wean
The process and people that it should protect
Mishandled and twisted from founding deflect

The promises null for it's just a ploy
To rack up the numbers opponents destroy
The people exist when it's time to vote
And they'll take the seat themselves they'll promote

A system that's broken but proud it still stands
Losing the value of blood on the land
Forgetting the justice the pledge of the old
The battles once won integrity sold

The cries of the people the country is lost
Replaced with ideals at such extreme costs
While policies failing united no more
Destruction within and terror takes shore

The government fighting the people distraught
Its enemies laughing at what they have wrought

THE PEOPLE'S GOVERNMENT Part 2

Political lies fly through the air
Feeding the people the bull of despair

Economy flexing a muscle so weak
Beating the masses with paychecks that wreak
The havoc of hunger while poverty maims
Releasing the anger of those brought to shame

Identities lost they can't pay their bills
Collection and repo and tax take their fill
While health is an issue they promise more lies
To give them a system to help them survive

Or give them some more of what feeds their pride
Eating poor pockets enjoying the ride
Political hands and lips stained with green
To function the system and hide the unseen

They ravage the people and band-aid their wounds
For honesty fails because they're immune
The country is dying division alive
Agendas self-serving with power connive

The crumbling vision fore-fathers protected
The documents eaten by worms greed perfected
The country the country the red white and blue
Redemption unseen the fabric torn through

TRAPPED
They don't know
I'm trapped inside
Fighting to be free

Defending truth
From judgements eyes
Intently scourging me

Born a lie
The outside view
Perceived to be the fact

But inside out
Is who I am
Existence can't retract

The crowded skin
I bare is tight
Holding back the pain

Living life
To please the mass
My happiness is feign

To open wide
The door of light
A place for pride to stand

And no more shame
Or hidden truths
Exposure would demand

Exist in peace
For who I am
And not what is believed

A freedom fair
But tough to gain
Identities bereaved

A lie is good
When comfortable
It makes the hearing ears

While others fade
Or drift away
In flooded lakes of tears

For in this world
The life of truth
Can bring a damning wind

To knock you down
Or take your breath
And push you to rescind

For now the doors
Are closed and locked
For fear of what may rise

When one is brave
And turns the knob
To open what belies

THE BLACKNESS
For the skin that he bares is an enemy
Though the reason isn't fair but it's plain to see
Being black is a threat to humanity
Killing brothers is a justified insanity

If he stands on the corner it's imprisonment
He can't smile at a lady and be innocent
When he walks great suspicion surely imminent
Shows emotion
Faces judgement and called insolent

For the color of his skin they will apprehend
If he runs a revolver will be how it ends
To the shame of the truth bullets now defend
Second chances don't exist
Death will make amends

Is it chance this is truth inadvertently
Are they victims of a complex conformity
Is it all in their minds or a certainty
To be black and a male—a monstrosity

FRIENEMY

Missiles flying in the air
Strength and fear is what they bare
Looking fierce to all below
Dominance is what they show

Gritting teeth and secret smiles
Shaking hands for miles and miles
Crossing fingers while they talk
Pass provisions as they walk

Sanctions prick with no reward
Cancelled by the veiled accord
Kiss the cheek and stab behind
Friend and foe are close aligned

SLAVERY

There is nothing for this man only misery
Though his birth was a true line of royalty
Whisked away by a selfish infirmity
To be chained and degraded egotistically

Take his roots and his pride call him less than man
Take his wife and his kids so he'll understand
There is nothing he can do only take the brand
For his life has the value of a grain of sand

Strip him down on the block for the world to see
He's a prize to the field sold as property
In his shame he will learn of his dignity
He's a species not compared to humanity

If he runs or rebels it's a whipping then
It's a message to the others master wants to send
To respect and obey those that apprehend
Disagree and a noose will be how it ends

From the sweat of his brow he will give his all
For the benefit of those in the future falls
From the melody of voices freedom often calls
To the ones who'll be brave to destroy the walls

In his hands there is power and authority
In his heart there is faith hope and charity
With his mind he can conquer every enemy
With his drive he can fly high successfully

Though his life poorly used by another man
Will be light to the struggle of another plan
And his legacy will trail and be greater than
Gaining victory through heirs in a lifespan

WHITE REFLECTION
He looks for peace
But has none to share
Justice demanded
With actions unfair

Pay him the debt
Society owes
Past hurt a weapon
He viciously throws

I am a victim
He often repeats
While killing his own
And blaming the streets

Stuck in a mindset
That we are to blame
Living in violence
Destroying with flames

Drugs sex and guns
His glorious mix
Honesty fails
Cause he's full of tricks

Arrogant rants
Of what he can do
Blood is a witness
To what he'll pursue

Why even bother
To give him a hand
He'll waste the time
And make more demands

If his life matters
As he oft proclaims
He'd honor the law
There'd be no more game

His lifestyle would change
Productive he'd be
But chances are slim
Cause he fails to see

The blame is his own
The choices he made
Brought on his despair
Himself he betrayed

EXCLUSION

Exclusion
An agent of suicide
Trying to hide
The reason one is denied
Presence
Acknowledgement that they exist
A smile
A Hi
Not body language that resists
The notion that one is there
Except for the snickers and stares
Degrading the breath breathed
Denying the space one occupies
So what one is fat or shy
Strange or poor
No one deserves to be ignored
The silence speaks volumes
The back turned creates wounds
Deeper than eyes can see

Or hearts can feel
Tormented for having to deal
With being alone
In a world so full
Time can't atone
For the lasting sweep
'Cause the scars cut deep
Rejection's silent persistence
Creating a world of distance
Losing hope and heart
Emotions torn apart
The voice once heard
Drowning in lost words
Smothered in a vastness of contusions
Administered by the hand of
Exclusion

MURDEROUS DEVOTION

Pushed to the edge of nothing
A final decision to end all
Shielded eyes from blood spilled
A hardened heart for what will befall

Torn and crushed by torment within
Angered for the lack of resolve
Drawn to the peace of quieted voices
With lifeless bodies the pressure dissolves

Question the motive buried alive
Twisted love and shattered emotion
Reasons once clear before the destruction
Murder the answer to brutal devotion

SHADOW MEN
Black silhouettes
Armed with color
Danger in the site of men

Black silhouettes
Guilty Innocence
Endangered for the thought of them

Black silhouettes
Good or bad
Death the sure reckoning

Black silhouettes
Kiss the ground
Lifeless color never threatening

BEYOND THE WALLS

Dreaming is dangerous where we live
Be sure to agree with those in power
We must walk the line and pay our homage
Or the little we have they will devour

We fear for our children day and night
Walking to school a hazardous mission
No laughter no play or trips to the park
But hovering near a timeless tradition

Each day we wake a blessing and curse
We hide in the places we should be free
The war destroying all that we have
Our homes are chapels to pray and grieve

Food is scarce for clean water we thirst
But plenty is poverty despair and grief
We witness lost hope unwarranted death
For innocent blood there is no relief

No jobs no money or substance to live
Many are driven to violent survival
Afraid for each moment to come and to pass
As peace and safety's a fluent deprival

So...

With little in hand we leave dreadful dark
Uncertainty sure but looking ahead
While void of regret we run from the worst
To places where dreams and hopes are well fed

REASONABLE ANGER

Afraid today may be my last
Deadly shadows the light has cast
On those that look like me
What we drive what we wear
It's always suspect
Even when we do our best to project
I'm cool I'm innocent doing nothing wrong
There's a stigma that belongs
"To Us"
The type that causes all to distrust
Beware
Be very aware
When you come into our presence
Fear follows and brings dissidence
Singled out surely bad news
From their point of view
There can't be something good
Coming from one that lives in the hood
...Or even the suburbs
Cause our residence
Doesn't change the precedence
That's been set by suspect murders
Even if we fail to comply
Do we all deserve to die

(next page)

It's like they see with a sentence in mind
No judge no jury no due process
So in fear
Some of us run
Cause we're not under arrest
We're under distress
Distressed that today may be the day
When our mothers and wives shed tears
Over a body that will no longer draw near
For a hug or a kiss
Distraught by the actions of those in authority
For their perception of minorities
Second class
We're no class at all
When funerals are the perpetual mass
Not a celebration of life
But a gathering for the slaughtered
Cause our lives have been bartered
For the satisfaction of our non-existence
And they wonder why we're angry
Why we're mad
The indifference to our plight
Yes we matter
But they shield their hearts
We're like meat on a platter
For dogs to feed
Their appetite has turned to greed
For the need
Of black lives to cease
Anger
Yes that's the emotion
When some have a devotion

To permanently quiet black voices
No sympathy no apology no justice
Our cries are buried deep
Beyond the dirt where death worms creep
The verdict never changed
Social media just broadened the range
For all to see
What was happening quietly
It's now loud and clear
But eyes default to naught
No matter why no matter what
We are a target
There's no shame for their harvest
Of black lives
Always was
Perpetual past
And it's happening so fast
So yes I'm angry
'Cause today could be my last

LOVE DIVIDE

I do - so fondly
The ease of words undone
Never becoming one
Wanting what exists in a single mind
Perception twisted by selfish visions
Joy deferred by undiscovered truths

For better or worse
A well-intended curse
Ignorant desire and heart
A knot tied with sparkling sunshine
Kissing perpetual bliss and rainbows
Fading color denying the wind and rain

'Til death us do part
Lies and broken words
Spilling emotional desire
Fires ignited doused with discontent
Moving to fantasies imagined soon to part
Death won't separate a love never found

POLITICAL IMPOTENCE

In and out opinions change
Dangling hope of false intent
Groping for agreeing minds
Teasing with a truth that's bent

Kissing faces just exchange
Tongues are lashing lying fair
Piercing through a broken past
Fingers stroking laws that tear

Heated talks of goals abhorred
Embracing cheats that smile and give
Holding measures selfish gain
Failing functions pressed to live

BLOODY DIRECTION

The bullet left the gun
We all better run
Beware duck and hide
Before the deadly collide

The shooter didn't aim
Or call somebody's name
The trigger pull was free
To choose all randomly

The bullet left the gun
We all better run
Beware duck and hid
Before the deadly collide

The beating of the heart
The bullet takes its start
No eyes to see the range
No feet to make a change

The bullet left the gun
We all better run
Beware duck and hide
Before the deadly collide

It pierces fast and strong
Its pain felt hard and long
No fear or tears it sheds
For those that fled or'r dead

The bullet left the gun
We all better run
Beware duck and hide
Before the deadly collide

NO CHARGE

A body and a face
His will does make the chase
As hands and eyes do stray
She fights to keep away

Invading secret spaces
Her heart does skip and races
He doesn't stop or pause
For damage he will cause

Just takes what's not his own
And leaves her there alone
Lost and sick within
She cannot stand her skin

The traces that he left
The water will take theft
Her voice they won't believe
He'll practice to deceive

She'll cry to no avail
He'll triumph without fail
He'll walk with conscious clear
She'll walk and dream in fear

A life that's full he'll lead
For her his choice impedes
So silence is her cause
Her rape becomes her flaws

On him the sun does shine
For her the darkness blinds
Creating so much pain
She carries it in vain

So where's the justice then
Or privileged are the men
A violation parted
So many take light-hearted

LIKE NO OTHER
Trumpets sounding
System surprised
Some are afraid
It's our countries demise

Never held office
But standing tall
Electoral College
The writing on the wall

Klan and supremacist
Speaking proud
Claiming the victory
In light – out loud

Nothing is usual
A sheer upset
Political division
But all rules met

Popular votes
A reverse of the read
The people decided
But old systems lead

Dead but still voters
They claim is the cause
The rigging of numbers
Has failed in applause

The woman was booted
Though polls were quite sure
She'd capture the win
The past she'd endure

Emails and scandals
Were spread like the wind
Truth and white lies
They could not rescind

Taxes and fraud
The hand that she played
Words from his mouth
Were weapons she laid

Sexual predator
Enemy's friend
Bigot and chauvinist
More to no end

Harsh and cold words
Were traded non stop
Frustration and hatred
A constant back drop

The trumpet still sounded
And brought a divide
Deepening passions
At home and world-wide

History made
Rejoicing and cheer
Are mingled with anger
Lost hope doubt and fear

IN CONTRAST
Bare feet and shoes with worn souls
Ragged clothes dirty bodies adorn
Scruffy hair scalped with dandruff old
Fingers stiff nails dirty and torn

Boxes and blankets a city does makes
Tents the luxury in the world of need
Carts and plastic bags possessions waste
Hunger thirst and want a perpetual deed

Closets full of shoes never to be worn
Silk satin and fur draping softened skin
Glistening strands salon perfect tresses
Manicured nails with a perfect trim

Mansions gated a city of their own
More the luxury when one never needs
Expensive cars and leather bags carry
A thirst for wealth the perpetual feed

A GREAT NATION

One nation under God
On whom they all stood
Founded moral and noble laws
Banded together a creation powerful
A nation's birth with infallible hopes to be

The promises from its trust
Deemed to secure its existence
And guarantee generational successes
Strength beyond destruction and blood shed
Bringing alive the future and dreams for all humanity

BEGIN AGAIN

After the rain comes the glistening sun
Wrapped in a rainbow of color and cheer
Birds sing the song of life and praise
Thanking the father for promises kept dear

Clean is the air washed by the storm
A subtle wind blows caressing the leaves
Sky full of blue and white cotton fluff
The flowers they wave and clap in the breeze

Creatures are dancing in puddles with joy
Gallops heard thunderous an earthly ovation
Parents are watching as children amuse
Life beckons sure a wondrous coronation

NATIVE DESTINY

Systematic extermination
Recapturing nightmares in distant memory
Washed by hands stained with blood
Deliberate destruction of one deemed an enemy

Polluted waters forcing all to drink
Perceptions twisted by fork tongued officials
Ethnic cleansing the manifest destiny
Hopes fulfilled by actions prejudicial

One pure race deemed to set the pace
Fixated to wipe a world created clean
Domination and slavery a fitted alternative
A dark side bright for the future seen

Blistered and wounded the state never healed
Freedom by pen strokes fading fast
Barely remembered the motives to fight
Destroying the present repeating the past

Legacy and truth destroyed in a moment
Pillage the tragedy of hate and divide
The theory that was is in fact correct
Future results past and present collide

Footsteps in puddles of unknown sorrow
Promises spoken but never attained
Tombs filled with hope and dreams never found
Heirs heard in whispers of life never gained

KEEP HOPE

Don't stop believing 'cause change is coming
You've come too far to give up now
The hope you've felt is still inside you
Don't close the curtains don't take a bow

Take every moment to aide your dreams
The steps you've made are not in vain
The day will come when persistence wins
And all your lack will turn to gain

LOST AT HOME

Lost in a familiar place
My loved ones surround me
Embraces and kisses not quite enough
To shed the haze that surrounds me

I know where I am and where I belong
But uncertainty clouds my mind
I want so much to enjoy this life
But the will I cannot find

I stand alone in a crowded room
They're blind to what's within
My functions fixed on autopilot
Feeling hurt but still frame a grin

BEHIND THE LINES

Wars are waging
And people are dying
Humanity grips the heart
But security beckons no

Freedom sings the song
That peace and safety may not hear
Lines in the earth a barrier
Cross or forced to stay

Voices plead relief
And voices speak the danger
Death marches in pools of blood
As eyes watch behind guarded walls

LOST

Circled paths and winding roads
Foggy vision and heavy loads
Lost and found and lost again
Searching for beginnings end

Twisted steps and windswept prints
Darkened lights and faded scents
Puzzling signs and shredded maps
Familiar scenes from time collapse

Confusion grand and hope is less
Dreams are void and nights unrest
Help seems far in drowning tears
Faith is eaten by doubt and fear

Silence voiced and screaming thoughts
Bleeding hearts from choices sought
Beaten strength and blistered will
Lost has won with time to fill

AWAY DEMOCRACY
Turn your foot democracy
Your worth is counted with disdain
Spread your wings in other lands
And reap the sight of death and pain

Your truth and way are not for all
The people's voice is spoke by one
Loosened chains are comfort there
A system praised and yours they shun

BEAR BEWARES

There once was a bear that lived regal
Who dreamed of a lion and eagle
The eagle he ate
The lion sat wait
He woke with a plan sly and lethal

CHOICES
Ninety nine or one
A crowd or all alone
Bouquet or single rose
A choice or none of those
The top or bottom feed
In plenty or in need
The stars or on the ground
For joy or sadness found

A PRESENT PAST

Present souls salute past torments
Freedom rings for only a moment
Voices rage a pale supremacy
Hate and violence granted clemency

Lost expressions finding life
Piercing those they once brought strife
Oppression stands and capes imposters
Adding fear to victim's roster

Death and tears defeat resistance
Chains do rattle in the distance
Hope is gathered by extremist
Glory's blood with pride persists

HOPELESS TIME

Broken bodies back again
Toiling futures drifting far
Precious faith a fading memory
Reaching for the falling star

Hallelujah victory's pain
Giving all to useless gain
Hallelujah fainting fast
Lifeline short and weak to cast

Tired feet a stumbling woe
Hands are stiffened holding not
Hearts are skipping beating less
Minds that bend to dreadful plots

Hallelujah victory's pain
Giving all to useless gain
Hallelujah fainting fast
Lifeline short and weak to cast

Arms that reached have fallen so
Singing now a dreadful cry
Peace has shifted torment's way
Darkness waits for light to die

Hallelujah victory's pain
Giving all to useless gain
Hallelujah fainting fast
Lifeline short and weak to cast

STROKES OF PAIN

Fighting for surrender
Hands stretching beyond their reach
Splintered souls weep in dismay
Voices cry out to be heard

Distant fears become familiar
Stroking pens of mass destruction
Streets are beaten with angered feet
Ears flare up to raging words

Melting pots are shards of glass
Drafted fences spark disdain
Freedom drifts in pools of tears
Hurt recalling torments past

Beaconed refuge dimmed by caution
Safety clouds the islands call
Lives are ripped and worlds are torn
Pain to see how long it lasts

SCRAMBLED LINES

Faith is twisted by convictions
Far beyond the founding line
Meshed within extreme devotion
Love declares the first design

Religion blamed for peace and war
Gods and spirits deemed a threat
Man declares creations own
Theories place their souls in debt

Truth believed is watered down
Democratic morals change
Will defies what fastened life
Faith and fear a close exchange

PRECIOUS FOOL
A fool's disgrace
In care or haste
Food time and money
A precious waste

ALLEGIANCE

Pledging allegiance to the wars
The waving waged within the shores
Symbolizing freedoms hand
Liberty stretched across the land

Pledging the colors lasting touch
Suffering fellows hated so much
Cursed upon the land they sowed
Hoping for reparations owed

Pledging to the stars of white
Taking hold with all their might
Pure and right with all they gained
Left behind the souls they stained

Pledging to the blood that shed
Equal worth alive or dead
Faithful fights for rights to be
Equal under sovereignty

CONFLICTS

Hatred declaring historic proprieties
Terror surviving and strengthened in piety
Love and religion inducing anxiety
Color and race invoking dubiety

Desires rejecting the role of sobriety
Political factions obtain notoriety
Unbalanced scales tipping societies
Double standards in one color varieties

GAS BY TRAGEDY

Taken for granted
The air that was breathed
Nostrils and lungs
Without thought fill with ease

Innocent souls
Take the day as the norm
Trusting the moments
Will come without harm

But lurking above
Is an abnormal wind
The strong and the brave
Won't prevail to defend

Quiet death creeping
The air that they trust
Betrayed by a figure
Corrupt and unjust

Sweeping the roads
Taking all by surprise
The young and the old
And the feeble and wise

Lifeless they've fallen
The weapon took hold
Others are gasping
To death they will fold

Shadows and questions
From pain left behind
Lost in a world
Who with evil's entwined

RAGING STORMS

Quiet storms that once rested in the belly of liberty
Have broken free from their chains
By which they were bound
The sacredness of peace
Between the peoples on the shores
Are disrupted by the
Manifestation of vain imaginations

Melting pots once flowing
With a united diversity
Have frozen in the heat
Of prejudice and entitlement
The legs of freedom once
Chased strong and proud
Have buckled in the memory
Of a not so distant past

Separation and degradation
Fulfill dreams of a dark future
Standing in uncertainty with
Rampant hate and violence
The halls of justice
Once revered grounded and fair
Have been crumbled in
Explosive battles of partisan pride

Lightning flashes fear
Thunder destroys silence
Rain drowns hope the wind uproots foundation
Shadows stand in the door of the heart of humanity
Peace pride and patriotism lost in a raging storm

CHANGE OF HEART
Shifted beauty shifted love
What once was good not good enough
Light now darkened hope declined
What once was shared is now assigned

THE MADNESS
The struggle for power will end in tragedy
The rungs on the ladder made of you(s) and me(s)
Crushing the value of humanity
Reaching the top will bring insanity

Killing their own unjustifiably
Wipe out existence they call enemy
Will leave them alone for no one else to see
Their hunger fulfilled self-inflicted depravity

REIGNING DARK DAYS

Default is darkness mischief hidden in the shadows
Secrets parade in their fullness nakedly unashamed
Lust has no fear or understanding of restraint

Lies and deceit the call of nature blowing in the wind
Greed licks its blood stained fingers with smirking lips
Pride has no urge to care for another

Malice and hate dance under the ever present moon
Bitterness floods the sky and releases a stinging rain
Anger has no use for words of wisdom

Eyes do wander and feet run to dangerous pleasures
Wrath walks thunderously with feet prepared for war
Corrupt are their ways no place for guiding light

BUCKETS AND BOATS
Struggle to stay afloat
In a boat full of holes
Bailing the water
With buckets they stole

Water once peaceful
Is now forcing in
The boat giving way
And the bucket's no friend

INDECENT BEHAVIORS
Second chances
Innocent until proven guilty
Accusations kill character and career

Long ago
Past behaviors contemptable
Present day outstanding and revered

Quieted voices
Empowered by the many
Breaking a silence enslaved by fear

Proof estranged
Victim's evidence in memory
Time washed reality tangible and near

Shaded truths
Possibilities left and right
Victims and predators on either side

Acceptable behavior
Power defined its strength
Opportunity stretching far and wide

Narratives revealed
Broken shackles hit the ground
Lifted voices the portal toward freedom

Society's woes
Breaking through the veils
Determined to find those who'll heed them

SILENCE OF THE MAN

An uncomfortable position when man is abused
His own masculinity often used
As a weapon to keep him silent and poised
He dare not make mention he dare not make noise
Of harassments, intrusions, violations endured
He won't be believed he won't be secured
Perceptions and culture refuse him the ease
To voice he's a victim to share what he sees
He's seen as a culprit no one could invade
His status as man brings views of him grayed
And so in the darkness he suffers alone
Ashamed of the pain that he quietly owns

SEXUAL ENTITLEMENT
A body and a face he thinks
She wears for his pleasure
The moment she steps into any space
Is his chance to harass beyond measure
Because of her lips and her "back stash"
Her mind disregarded
She's treated second class
In a world he thinks is his own
His hands do wander and his eyes do roam
To her breast he imagines a lustful home
His words cut her spirit demeaning integrity
To go along and play his game
He assures prosperity
A tool a toy a piece of meat on his plate
His vile intensions dangling authority as the bait
A man yes he is and that entitlement
Grants him permission
With winks and smiles
He practices the age old tradition
Harmless he says
Oh she asked for this attention
But her resistance and her fear
He thoughtfully didn't mention
So she's left in the darkness
All alone and scared to speak
And he parades and thumps his chest
And another victim he seeks
The world has tipped its hat
At the women in the dirt
And the men receive its praise
As their hands are up a skirt

THE NEVER ENDING STORY
Black tigers and white dragons
Fighting fiercely for their own
Debating times and ancient spaces
Of the air and earth they roam

Consuming fires deadly claws
Leaving carnage on their pride
Death opposes both their futures
But in hope they still collide

ADDICTED
Battled and bewildered
Pain bringing more pain
Addicted to the chronicles of life

The joys of misery
Lifted beyond
Substitutions for emotional strife

Engaging war
In the heart of their minds
Finding solace in an artificial peace

Illusions of confusion
Twisted realities
High is the place of release

Smoke screens in paper
Bottles cans and pipes
Poisons with a happy face

Needles and straws
Dependent friends
Transporting to a happy place

A circle of life
High then low
With a mixture of pride and regret

Broken and free
In a mind not their own
Take the value their substance has set

GOVERNMENT'S DEPENDENCY

Too much government deemed
Service to the people
Consequences fatal
And future full of deep holes

Dependency the back hand
No search for something better
Hands will always reach out
And milk it to the letter

Able bodies maintained
Don't see a reason to change
Lined up and wanting more
A lifestyle that's prearranged

Harvest weakened abilities
When aid requires no return
Broken plans solutions wane
Conditioned minds will always yearn

ABORTION
Life existence debated in question
Purpose beginning the matter conception
Emotions desires committing the treason
Knowledge and wisdom consider the reasons

Choices and voices demanding the law
Religion and morals exposing the flaws
Professions confessions revealing disgust
Killing a vision for passion and lust

Neglected protections unbalanced in mind
A forceful intrusion a seed left behind
Decisions and anguish the left and the right
Defending the heartbeat or bid it goodnight

Life existence debated in question
Purpose beginning the matter conception
Emotions desires committing the treason
Knowledge and wisdom consider the reason

LEFT BEHIND
Running from despair into fiery flames
Present worlds colliding and the past is to blame
The future hiding out with no will to appear
Desperate souls are crying under pressure and fear

Light is casting shadows bringing doubt to the front
Darkness is prevailing leaving victims in want
Blood becoming water the desire for greed
Innocence and weakness the perpetual feed

Survival to the fittest with the mind to connive
Devoted to the mission for its species to thrive
Strength is in the evil that has taken the horn
Creations moral pulse is instinctively torn

Sightless is the vision with the powerful hands
Beating freedom senseless with its selfish demands
Sovereignty devoted to adulterous abuse
Outraged is the banner for its treacherous use

FAITH AND PATRIOTISM

For the love of God and country
Arms reach out to lend a hand
Hearts are driven by a pure love
Spreading hope across the land

For the love of God and country
Every human is a friend
And the differences within all
Won't become truths to defend

For the love of God and country
Faith expands in every heart
Reaching far beyond the vision
Convincing all to do their part

For the love of God and country
All are proud of freedom's fame
And the deeds that are accomplished
Bare the proof of her great name

For the love of God and country
Fear is conquered by accord
Peace and strength will grow and nourish
For a future well secured

LOVE SURVIVES

It can survive a storm of raging words
A shattered heart from an untrue lover
It protects the weak and gives its all
Meer faults its passion grants to cover

It stares the face of fear head on
(The) Unknown is beaten by its strength
It gently breaks the toughest will
It grants integrity time and length

Darkness fades upon its touch
It lifts the bowed down head with ease
It opens arms and changes minds
It satisfies and aims to please

It chastens wrong with pure intent
It judges not opposing hands
It waits with patience to be seen
It causes right to take a stand

Sometimes - rejection's what it gets
Its presence wrongfully accused
It goes unnoticed near and far
Its generosity abused

Hatred contradicts its cause
Lies are told to hide its light
The weight it carries conquers all
But still *it* thrives and stands to fight

Life and death applaud its skill
Wisdom crowned it from conception
Peace is found within its bosom
It blesses all upon reception

Rise and fall and rise again
Keeping hope alive my friend
Pressing onward to the light
Reaching for the highest height

THE END

www.ingramcontent.com/pod-product-compliance
Lightning Source LLC
Chambersburg PA
CBHW051807040426

42446CB00007B/554